REFLECTIONS

A Pursuit of God's Lessons in the Field

JEFF VORDERMARK

WESTBOW
PRESS®
A DIVISION OF THOMAS NELSON
& ZONDERVAN

Scripture quotations taken from the New American Standard Bible˚, Copyright © 1960, 1962, 1963, 1968, 1971, 1972, 1973, 1975, 1977, 1995 by The Lockman Foundation. Used by permission. (www.Lockman.org)

WestBow Press books may be ordered through booksellers or by contacting:

WestBow Press
A Division of Thomas Nelson & Zondervan
1663 Liberty Drive
Bloomington, IN 47403
www.westbowpress.com
1 (866) 928-1240

Original artwork by Logan Hathaway

ISBN: 978-1-4908-8215-4 (sc)
ISBN: 978-1-4908-8216-1 (hc)
ISBN: 978-1-4908-8214-7 (e)

Library of Congress Control Number: 2015908637

Print information available on the last page.

WestBow Press rev. date: 07/07/2017

Dedicated to my high school English teacher, who possessed the gift of encouragement. Thanks, Pat—you made a difference!

Contents

Introduction

I spent some time one Sunday morning not too long ago caring for a friend who was no longer able to attend church. Age and Parkinson's disease had robbed him of his ability to communicate well, but that did not stop us from worshipping together. The wonders of modern technology, via cable, brought church to us on a flat-screen TV. We listened while Pastor David Jeremiah delivered his weekly missive.

The pastor shared the story of an atheist who had challenged God to a "man-making" contest. I'd never heard this story before, so it captured my immediate attention. The atheist, steeped in the findings of modern science, was a bit full of himself, especially since mankind seemed on the verge of being able to clone a human being. He thus feels empowered to challenge God—who accepted.

The atheist said, "We'll do it the old-fashioned way," and reached down to grab a handful of dust from the ground. The story ends there, as God resolved the entire issue by saying simply, "Wait a minute, go get your own dirt."

As a hunter and outdoorsman, I am reminded that nothing we do in God's natural world happens without God having had a hand in it. If I find the right tree to place a stand, it is because in God's natural order of things, that's where He placed the tree. If there is forage available for the animals I pursue, it's not because I took it upon myself to provide it. God did. Even the presence of game itself is not something I have the wherewithal to make happen. God in His active creation of the universe put this all into motion. It is with this mind-set that I go forth into field and forest—my "wilderness." It is in this wilderness, I honor the Creator by enjoying His creation, His bounty, and His teachings.

1

Into the Wilderness

The kingdom of heaven is like a merchant seeking fine pearls, and upon finding one pearl of great value, he went and sold all that he had and bought it. (Matthew 13:45–46)

"Everything That Glitters Is Not Gold" is a song written by Dan Seals and Bob McDill. It says, "And, oh the crowd will always love you. But as for me I've come to know everything that glitters is not gold." Everything that glitters is not gold; this is a key refrain from an all-time favorite song. The older I get, the more I come to realize just how true this rings. It seems our version of gold today centers on the stock markets in New York. We hear daily about Wall Street, what the closing averages were, and which stocks were winners and losers. But Wall Street is for most a false promise, empty glitter, costly confetti. The book of Revelation presents a very different take on the matter of riches: "I advise you to buy from Me gold refined by fire so that you may become rich, and white garments so that you may clothe yourself, and *that* the shame of your nakedness will not be revealed; and eye salve to anoint your eyes so that you may see" (Revelation 3:18, emphasis added). This gold is something not available in the stores of man, so if you happen to be looking in the vicinity of Wall Street, you will always be off the mark.

Perhaps instead of looking to Wall Street, we should look to the wild places for the gold that only God can offer. Consider for just a moment the gold in the morning sunrise or the gold in a spiderweb that catches and reflects diamonds of brilliance. Then you can begin to understand that God stores treasures for us all in the wilderness. Sometimes, for such glimpses to be revealed, we don't even need to be out of cell phone contact but just off the beaten path and ready to see. But some may fear what they find in that wilderness, where escaping the voice of God can be difficult since the option of burying ourselves in everyday pursuits is not available. Perhaps that is why we should go out there and face it, just as Jesus did.

Jesus did more than just go to His wilderness. He was nearly lost in it, having come face-to-face with the Adversary, and by doing so provided us a clear reminder of how harsh any wilderness can be. Yet He was ready, having lived a life of preparation to be able to meet the spiritual challenges He would face. He was God's own, prepared from a life of testing for what would be His supreme challenge: the temptation by Satan. None of us are immune to Satan's efforts to steal the unwary from God's kingdom. It is a challenge we deal with all too often, and our success is certainly not guaranteed. Our ultimate example and highest hope is to know that although Jesus was sorely tested in the wilderness, He prevailed. Perhaps there are lessons for us out here too.

Do we need to allow ourselves to be called into the wilderness to separate the wheat from the chaff, this world from God's kingdom, and head knowledge from heart knowledge, just as Jesus did? Do you spend time in the outdoors to truly experience the wilderness? Do you go for the going or for something more?

We need to become lost in the wilderness just as Jesus was, going there with only what we can carry in, including the burdens of our thoughts, hopes, and desires. This is no place for a television set or car. To enter the wilderness is to escape these very things; the influences of this world should not reach into our wild places. This place, you see, is where we go to hear our hearts. So the next time you step foot into the wild, consider the cost of your current life, and see if you're up to the challenge of meeting God on His terms—not yours. Seek the pearl of great price, and get lost in God.

2

Good Habitat …and Bad

He was afraid and said, "How awesome is this place!
This is none other than the house of God, and this is
the gate of heaven." (Genesis 28:17)

I was excited about the prospects of hunting a new property,
but my first impression was not what I had envisioned. This
property had recently been bought by a friend, an army chaplain
stationed overseas. Imagine my surprise when I drove onto the
property through the opening where a gate used to be, got out
of the truck, and found this location to be a popular partying
spot for young men. (I figured it was not young women who left
remnants of the type of magazine I found lying on the ground
among the other litter that included a huge fire pit, broken liquor
bottles, and empty beer cans.) This marked a disappointing
introduction to the property, and I felt a twinge of personal
violation. The unguarded entry had been an invitation, and

presented a dilemma about what, exactly, to do since there was nobody present to guard the gates.

Despite my high hopes for this farm, that immediate impression stuck over the weeks to come. On subsequent visits, I took it upon myself to clean up everything since this property belonged to a Christian brother. Aside from a very small area of tainted habitat, the rest of the farm was exceptional. My son and I spent quite a few days on it over Christmas vacation and saw large numbers of deer, turkey, and rabbits. This was not the norm for other properties I had been hunting on, so it seemed like we had stumbled onto a bit of a heaven on earth. I even cut fresh bobcat tracks twice in two days, an altogether unusual event. Still, it bothered me that I had to clean up after others because, in a way, this wasn't just any habitat—it was now Christian habitat. I informed my friend via e-mail that I would do my best to perform duties as the watchman.

It is not just our physical holdings that we need to guard, though. That sense of violation lingered, and I found myself considering other instances in which things unbidden came through the gates of my life. I was forced to ask, what do I cultivate in the everyday habitat of my workplace and home? I have to admit that stuff gets in my gate that shouldn't. The Internet makes it too easy, and so does television. My home habitat is further plagued by unwanted phone calls from people trying to sell things I don't need to buy as well as my inability to leave secular problems at the workplace. I can do better, and so today that farm stands as a reminder to take care about what I let in my own gate. At the same time, I need to find trusted friends who will help me with the guard duties should my own focus fail. It is good to ensure someone is there to guard the gates and protect the habitat. After all, habitat is important—for animals and people alike.

3

Dipping a Line in Holy Water

> Therefore, brethren, be all the more diligent to make certain about His calling and choosing you; for as long as you practice these things, you will never stumble; for in this way the entrance into the eternal kingdom of our Lord and Savior Jesus Christ will be abundantly supplied to you. (2 Peter 1:10–11)

The stillness of the morning was broken only by the occasional sound of a trout sipping an insect off the surface of the calm mountain lake that lay before me. All was crisp and clear, with a lingering bite in the air that only comes from being at an extreme altitude during this time of year. The day was June 6, a day to be commemorated for what happened on the beaches of Normandy during that fateful day in 1944, but for me it was a day to be spent in solitude. Perhaps for a veteran this was a fitting way to mark the passing of this particular date. I had been afforded a rare opportunity for reflection and introspection and chose to face my circumstances with a fly rod in hand and an eye on the water for rising trout. *Perhaps today, I thought, the brookies and other local salmonids will find my offerings worthy.*

This lake—one of perhaps dozens if not hundreds like it in this region of Colorado—was set like an emerald jewel, the largest of three that lay like pendants in a necklace on the throat of this small canyon. The sun was still ascending but shining brightly at this point on one of the fourteeners, a name given to mountains that rise over fourteen thousand feet, of which there were fifteen in the area. The setting was exhilarating and inspiring—a feast for the eyes and senses.

From time to time the air rang with the strident call of a kingfisher eager for an early-morning meal. I'm sure it was that and not from any sense that I represented some sort of worthy competition. Kingfishers are among nature's more interesting oddities. They seem quick to protest your presence in their selected fishing areas and don't hesitate to dive bomb a choice target right next to you as if to say, like some peevish sibling, "I'll do what I like, and you can't stop me."

A hen mallard with her brood that I had seen on previous outings passed nearby in a silent waterborne processional, keeping one wary eye on me and another peeled for any other dangers as she did. I noted sadly that her brood was smaller, apparently having lost a member to some sort of predator, of which there were many in this remote place.

A muskrat also made a brief appearance. The furtive little creature seemed to prefer moving on the edges of my vision, like intuition lurks on the edge of your mind about something you can feel more than verify. Were it not for the wake of water he left as evidence, you might have been tempted to ask if he was even there at all. Certainly any trace of his passing was soon smoothed away.

The water itself was amazingly clear, and it was almost too tempting to set the hook on rising fish even before the telltale movement of my strike indicator. The fishing flowed seamlessly into a long period of catching. It almost seemed unfair; I was experiencing phenomenal luck and had caught a number of trout before too long. I was only a novice at trout on a fly, having spent most of my formative fishing years in the flatlands where bass and pan fish were the order of the day, but today I felt particularly capable and blessed. It all seemed magical and was just the sort of experience I had heretofore only dreamed of or perhaps read in a magazine article written by some other more fortunate soul I previously could only have imagined might have been prone to embellishment.

I was in the zone, as some would call it, having entered that special place where thought did not happen, reasoning was not necessary, and the tempo of my world was dictated by the movement of my rod and fighting of the fish. All else ceased to be, and somewhere in that moment of timelessness, God spoke to me. I knew God lived up here, the fact having been evident to me on virtually every occasion I had visited and in every event that occurred. The sheer beauty of the place bespoke a Creator. Only now, He had something to teach me, and for that moment my daily, worry-filled, and worldly life was suspended as I went to school at the feet of the Master. It occurred to me the exceeding clarity of the water was something only God could arrange and that the action had been generated for my benefit alone. I felt a kinship at that moment with the early Indians who roamed America long ago in a way that demonstrated so much respect for the animals that sustained them and for the Spirit they acknowledged in their beliefs.

I too felt as if God was just over my shoulder, asking "Jeff, consider that you are one of those fish, and the flies on the surface are blessings that I have provided for you. How do you get them?"

With a strange clarity that for the moment matched the water, I realized what the answer was. As God's children, we must move to His offerings for us and take hold of them. If we wait for the good stuff to float right to us with a favorable current, we might be waiting a long time. I thought of how often I had seen a good fish and cast to it, only to have my offering overlooked because my technique was poor or worse, rejected even with a good presentation. Did I do that with God? It was a simple yet sublime message.

I looked at the pond again, this time with a changed perspective. The rod had long since stopped moving, and my efforts at eliciting action with what I had fondly termed my magic wand had ceased. I noted that fish would just as easily move up as down to catch a bite and that some were more active than others. Hmmmm, did that mean blessings were all around us? And how about their activity levels ... or ours? Were some just more greedy than others? What did that say about me? Was I missing blessings or opportunities to serve? Did God want me to be more active?

I pondered the size of the fish I had caught that morning. There were certainly no monsters, and some were really quite tiny—five- or six-inch brookies, which couldn't manage much of a struggle on the equipment I was using. However, they put up the same fight, inch for inch, as even the largest fish I had managed to catch. Little blessings? You bet! I suddenly understood that all of us, just like the fish in any body of water, must participate in order to move ahead and grow. Size was not the issue; it was what you did with opportunity that mattered.

God had shared some special insight with me that morning. He wanted me to be active. He wanted me to be on the lookout for opportunities—big and small—and to do it as a matter of course, not when the mood arose or when I had carved time out of my schedule. I had dipped my line in holy water, and my catch was of surpassing and everlasting value.

I turned to go and at the top of the rise looked back for one last glance to cement the moment. All was as it had been when I arrived—the sun a little higher in the sky and the duck family merrily paddling about. The kingfisher was nowhere to be seen or heard, but that lake—somehow it looked different. It shone brighter than I remembered, perhaps because of my vantage point or perhaps because I had gained clarity of vision, which was just one more blessing on a perfect summer day.

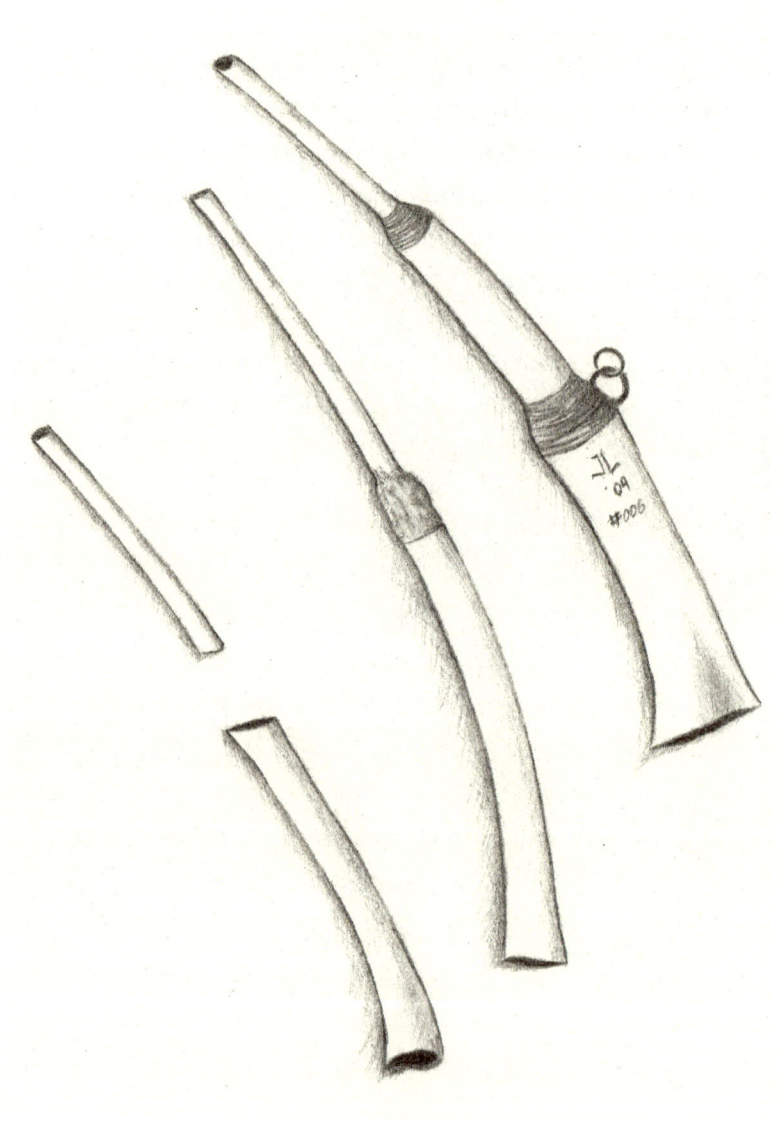

4

The Unfinished Call

David girded his sword over his armor and tried to
walk, for he had not tested *them*. So David said to
Saul, "I cannot go with these, for I have not tested
them." And David took them off. (1 Samuel 17:39)

It was my turn to make a morning announcement in chapel
concerning a new ministry our chaplain had asked me to start
up. I had purposed earlier in the week to bring one of the
finished turkey calls I had fashioned out of a real bird's wing
bones and hoped to enlist the help of a young protégé up in the
audience as I made the announcement. However, in my haste to
depart my workplace on Friday, I had forgotten my completed
calls in a locked office, irretrievable until Monday. That was
too late!

Of course, had I accomplished just a tiny bit of planning
prior to the day of the event, perhaps I could have avoided the
rapidly growing agony over my unpreparedness. The joke I

like to share with my own students about this very subject stole unbidden into my thoughts. "You know the difference between hard work and procrastination? Hard work pays off over time, but procrastination pays off right now!" I had accomplished exactly zero hard work in anticipation of the launch of this ministry. I looked around my home workshop for other finished calls but could find none. Instead I found a stash of calls in various stages of completion. By now I was running very late, so I grabbed one, stuck it in my Bible cover, and rushed out the door to the chapel.

I found myself working over my options as to how to get people's attention as I drove. With each passing minute, I seemed to be drawing closer to purgatory than God's house as I nervously anticipated the blank stares that were sure to greet my soon-to-be-evident lack of effort once I started babbling in front of four hundred congregants. After the twenty-minute trip, I was no closer to any sort of an idea, but I still didn't want my introduction to this ministry to be just another vanilla announcement. I had the unfinished call and the germ of an idea but not much beyond that. Showtime was moments away, and I foresaw a bland, "Yeah, this is going to happen on this date and time, and I sure hope to see you," introduction of the congregation to the new ministry despite my best efforts at crisis management. I certainly had not given God my best in preparation and felt appropriately convicted.

Genius struck as I waited in the rear of the chapel to be introduced, and it came in the form of the Holy Spirit. I thought about the unfinished call I had and realized that even though it was not perfect, it would still call a turkey. Oh sure, it still needed to have the glue seams smoothed and to be wrapped with colored thread (red and blue, of course, to go with the white bone—a patriotic theme) and fitted for a lanyard loop.

The final step of buffing the call so that it gleamed had not been accomplished. Neither had the call been tested in the field, but the tones had certainly sounded good in the garage. For all intents and purposes, it was a turkey call, just not a nice, finished product.

The Spirit showed me most Christians are just like that call. We become Christians at the moment we accept who Christ is and that He died for our sins. By making a willful decision to follow Him, we become new in Christ, a new creation. But we are certainly not tested. We are certainly not polished. And we certainly have not been wrapped in God's Word so it becomes a shield about us. We are all unfinished in that regard, and it takes years of submission to God's will for us to become truly refined.

It was this lesson, seared on my brain moments before I was to speak, that I shared with the congregation. They were not my words but God's lesson internalized. It represented another moment of shaping and preparation in my life as a Christian in preparation for eternity.

5

Seesaw ...

The hearing ear and the seeing eye, the LORD has made both of them. (Proverbs 20:12)

I saw beauty today. It is the same beauty you have seen if you've ever been afield at first light. The nighttime stars fade as dawn begins to cast its will upon the land. Light charges in and illuminates your surroundings, lifting form out of darkness and substance out of void. Shadows themselves are given the illusion of movement, animated by the flood of light and increasing brilliance of color that materializes like a painting out of the gray haze of predawn.

This one lingering yet exquisite moment in time forced me to stop and ponder what was happening. This simple moment, both sublime and brilliant, was to be cherished. An exultant flash of beauty had screamed of a singular grace and glory. It was a moment that could only be truly appreciated if one acknowledges that, above all else, it came because the hand of a Master was wielding the brush.

I saw such beauty today because I took the time to reflect, and in that pause I came to understand I was indeed both fearfully and wonderfully made. I was a man crafted in God's own image, a fellow heir of God's vast creation and thus able to appreciate on physical, spiritual, and emotional levels that this moment was not one simply of nocturnal versus diurnal or predator versus prey.

I was made to see that only that piece of creation made in God's likeness—mankind—could perceive, internalize, and be inspired by the majesty of what was seen. It was this truth that made me at once immensely humble and happy, like a child receiving a simple but unmerited gift that in its giving said very clearly, "You are valued, and you are loved." Putting on the eyes of a child of God, now was the time to appreciate the moment and gain a glimpse into the kingdom.

I saw beauty today. I saw because I purposed to see, to remove false filters of earthly distraction I cannot change and worldly circumstances I cannot fix, all the while defying an earthly view that claims beauty is defined not by an ever-changing landscape to the glory of God but by man's own definition. This is a strident, grating demand that what is seen can only be based on the true realities of science, accepted fact, and conventional wisdom. The beauty I saw outstripped them all and can freely be witnessed by all mankind because in the moment of our creation we were all given lifetime passes to the show. It is God's delight to offer these moments, and in turn we must attribute credit where it is due. The lens chosen to interpret these moments can, and will, frame our eternity.

As for me, it is no mystery that I saw beauty. I saw because I looked. I saw because I keep my eyes open, like a watchman on the tower, ever seeking evidence of God's dominion. I saw beauty today because I chose to see. I will see beauty again because I will purpose to find it. It is there. It is promised. Can you see it?

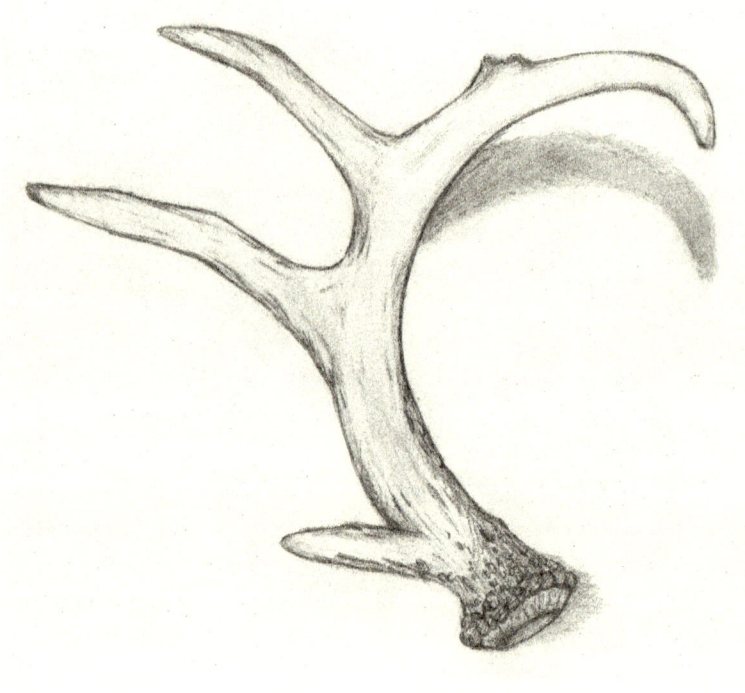

6

Sheds

Be anxious for nothing, but in everything by prayer
and supplication with thanksgiving let your requests
be made known to God. (Philippians 4:6)

Our basement is also our family room. My wife calls it the
DAD room, standing for "dead animal den." It is where I have
memories of some of my more successful trips afield. There's
not a lot hanging on the walls, but what is up there I'm pretty
proud of, all the more so because some of the taxidermy I've
actually done myself, including a huge mallard drake that has
survived seven different household moves and nine years of
storage intact since being taken in 1985. It's pretty neat to be
able to bring folks in your house and to be able to tell them,
"See those ducks on the wall? That's my work." I got a couple
of deer that I turned into European mounts and some pretty
nice turkey fans hanging around. However, one of my favorite

displays is saved for last in order to highlight my growing collection of deer antler sheds.

It's a great subject because one would be amazed at the number of people who do not realize deer lose their antlers every year or that while they are growing, deer antler represents one of the fastest-growing tissues known. When folks who have never seen a shed have the opportunity to actually hold one, it helps them better understand the animals they usually only see in fleeting glimpses on the side of the road.

But what is a shed antler really? For some it's an oddity found by sheer chance on a walk in the woods. For a few who know how to market a product that is valued as an Oriental herbal medicine or aphrodisiac, it represents a potential source of income. For others who enjoy looking for them, a shed found in the spring can tell a hunter which bucks made it through a tough winter, and finding a matched set off the same deer can represent a unique trophy to the collector. Those are rare, and in all my years of searching, I have never had the good fortune to find a set. But the shed itself is nothing more than a castoff. You see, once the rut is over and the deep of winter sets in, bucks no longer have a need to carry those bones on their heads. They are extra weight. In the lean times the weight makes them work harder, so to conserve energy, they cast them off.

The following spring the bucks will grow new ones, and depending on the age and condition of the animal, what results can be much more impressive than the headgear carried just a few months before. The sheds can be useful in other ways too. Rodents may gnaw on them for the calcium and the minerals they contain, or perhaps they will just weather away on the forest floor, returning their nutrients to the soil and in the meantime serve as a silent sentinel to mark the passing of the animal that bore them. Even better, perhaps I'll come along and find these little treasures before they weather away or are otherwise chewed into oblivion by the squirrels. Sheds normally do not last long once they are cast off, usually only a matter of months, so in order to find them, it is best to get out early, before Mother Nature does them in.

Shed hunting has become a bit of an addiction, a late-winter excuse to escape the confines of the house and enjoy an outing with the potential for a tangible reward. So whenever weather and free time permit, I will wander deer trails and known bedding areas in my search. I am fortunate even if I find only two or three sheds a year; that's enough to keep me coming back for more. I'm not really sure what I'll do with the sheds that now adorn a wrought iron wine rack in the DAD, but sometime down the road I'm sure I'll figure out a use for them aside from conversation pieces.

In the meantime I've come to ponder the meaning of sheds. I believe every once in a while we need to take stock of our own lives and figure out what we're lugging around that just serves no useful purpose anymore. What needs to be cast off or throw down at the feet of God because it is no longer any good to us or is a burden that is weighing us down? I've come to realize that I don't need to go to the woods to go find a shed. Some days maybe it's just best to spend some time and do a little shed hunting in my own life and figure out what needs to go away.

They are things that we hang on to: insults, pains, unforgiveness, or any manner of perceived slights or wrongs by others that over time become useless baggage. Sometimes it is our habits, such as too much TV or one too many helpings at the dinner table. Sometimes it's stuff. I think we've all seen the shows about the hoarders who just keep accumulating more and more junk. They really do not need any of these items, and neither do they use any of it; they just have it for whatever reasons they have manufactured in their own minds.

I've come to appreciate that I do have some things in my life which are just not necessary, and I need to take the time to figure out what those are, like my sins and attitudes, and get rid of them. Those are perhaps the most important sheds that we can leave behind. We serve an accepting God, one who is more than willing to pick up the things in our lives that we need to cast off and place into His collection of forgiveness and grace. We can cast them down at God's feet, knowing that if there ever is a recurring need for any of them, He will provide. Sometimes, like those bucks that make it through, what He provides may even be bigger and better. Maybe it's time for you to do little shed hunting in your own life.

7

Wind Cannot Blow
Away a Shaft of Light

As a result, we are no longer to be children, tossed
here and there by waves and carried about by
every wind of doctrine, by the trickery of men, by
craftiness in deceitful scheming. (Ephesians 4:14)

Early-morning sunlight began to stream through the bare
branches of November trees following the final major leaf drop
of the fall season. The sunlight was a welcome visitor, taking
the edge off a biting north wind that at times seemed like it
might knock me off my small perch eighteen feet above a well-
used intersection of deer trails. My bow hung unused next to
me as my hands were thrust deep inside my pockets in a feeble
attempt to conserve body heat.

The warmth of the sunlight became most welcome on my
feet and legs, making the long, cold sit in the tree more bearable.

There was certainly no deer movement that served to warm me up, so I was left with only my own thoughts to contemplate. The wind blew steadily, but the sunlight was unaffected, continuing to warm me and to slowly raise the chilly fall temperatures. It made me think of the immutability of God's Word, which serves to illumine us in those moments when we care to make reflection count. The wind is earthly, steady, and constant, but it could in no way blow away the sunlight. In the same manner, God's truth—His light to us—remains unaffected.

Indeed, wind cannot blow away a shaft of light. Neither can worldly man's incessant attempts to define the indefinable via science or the rhetoric of justification blow away the power of a believer's faith and the light of God's Word. This insight was trophy enough for an otherwise unproductive day on the deer stand. I made my way back to the truck bathed in brilliant sunshine, paying no heed to the wind.

8

The Ultimate Outfitter

Finally, be strong in the Lord and in the strength of His might. Put on the full armor of God, so that you will be able to stand firm against the schemes of the devil. For our struggle is not against flesh and blood, but against the rulers, against the powers, against the world forces of this darkness, against the spiritual *forces* of wickedness in the heavenly *places*. Therefore, take up the full armor of God, so that you will be able to resist in the evil day, and having done everything, to stand firm. Stand firm therefore, HAVING GIRDED YOUR LOINS WITH TRUTH, and HAVING PUT ON THE BREASTPLATE OF RIGHTEOUSNESS, and having shod YOUR FEET WITH THE PREPARATION OF THE GOSPEL OF PEACE; in addition to all, taking up the shield of faith with which you will be able to extinguish all the flaming arrows of the evil *one*. And take THE HELMET OF SALVATION, and the sword of the Spirit, which is the word of God. *(*Ephesians 6:10–17)

I'm a turkey hunter. There is a ritual of preparation each time I enter the woods in the spring. It is virtually the same every time, thus conjuring up these verses out of Ephesians as I go about this ritual in the last hour of morning's darkness.

Instead of "girding my loins with the truth," however, I wrap myself in a pymethrin-doused ghillie suit in order to ward off ticks, which can be a real problem where I live. Since these little critters can transmit some nasty diseases, and altogether too many friends have Lyme disease as a result of a tick bite, you can bet I take their presence seriously. My "breastplate of righteousness" is in fact my trusty pack into which I can place all manner of calls and other equipment I might need for the hunt. My feet are shod not with the "preparation of the gospel of peace" but with something a bit more practical when wandering through wet morning grass and thick vegetation that can hide venomous reptiles. They are not numerous, but having had one of my dogs bitten a couple of years back, one can't be too careful. My "helmet of salvation" is my face mask, which shields my countenance from hordes of mosquitoes in the spring. Finally, instead of the "sword of the Spirit," the only offensive weapon mentioned, I carry a bow or a shotgun as my weapon of choice during these forays into the woods.

My ritual of preparation is likely shared by legions of turkey hunters who take to the woods in the spring, and we are all a bit like David of the Old Testament. *Meleagris gallopavo*, more commonly known as the wild turkey, was not native to the lands of ancient Israel. There were, however, other, much more dangerous animals to be concerned with. Wild turkeys will run or fly away from danger, but not so a wild bear or Asiatic lion, both of which were common in the region then. As we know from our readings of Scripture, David was very dependable and so could be counted on to go forth well prepared to protect the sheep of his father. I guarantee you he did not go unarmed. Neither did he confront Goliath the Philistine by going forth unprepared. He may have been characterized as young, but somebody taught him right.

First Samuel 17 records the story of David's confrontation with Goliath.

> David said to Saul, "Let no man's heart fail on account of him; your servant will go and fight with this Philistine." Then Saul said to David, "You are not able to go against this Philistine to fight with him; for you are *but* a youth while he has been a warrior from his youth." But David said to Saul, "Your servant was tending his father's sheep. When a lion or a bear came and took a lamb from the flock, I went out after him and attacked him, and rescued *it* from his mouth; and when he rose up against me, I seized *him* by his beard and struck him and killed him. Your servant has killed both the lion and the bear; and this uncircumcised Philistine will be like one of them, since he has taunted the armies of the living God." And David said, "The LORD who delivered me from the paw of the lion and from the paw of the bear, He will deliver me from the hand of this Philistine." And Saul said to David, "Go, and may the LORD be with you." Then Saul clothed David with his garments and put a bronze helmet on his head, and he clothed him with armor. David girded his sword over his armor and tried to walk, for he had not tested *them*. So David said to Saul, "I cannot go with these, for I have not tested *them*." And David took them off. He took his stick in his hand and chose for himself five smooth stones from the brook, and put them in the shepherd's bag which he had, even in *his* pouch, and his sling was

in his hand; and he approached the Philistine. Then the Philistine came on and approached David, with the shield-bearer in front of him. When the Philistine looked and saw David, he disdained him; for he was *but* a youth, and ruddy, with a handsome appearance. The Philistine said to David, "Am I a dog, that you come to me with sticks?" And the Philistine cursed David by his gods. The Philistine also said to David, "Come to me, and I will give your flesh to the birds of the sky and the beasts of the field." Then David said to the Philistine, "You come to me with a sword, a spear, and a javelin, but I come to you in the name of the LORD of hosts, the God of the armies of Israel, whom you have taunted. This day the LORD will deliver you up into my hands, and I will strike you down and remove your head from you. And I will give the dead bodies of the army of the Philistines this day to the birds of the sky and the wild beasts of the earth, that all the earth may know that there is a God in Israel, and that all this assembly may know that the LORD does not deliver by sword or by spear; for the battle is the LORD's and He will give you into our hands." (1 Samuel 17:32–47)

As we can see, David's preparation for his battle with Goliath was thorough, even declining the offer to wear Saul's armor even though you can be assured that, as Saul was king, his was the finest available. Some Bible versions say David was uncomfortable in the armor because he had not tested it. He confronted Goliath instead with the tools with which he was familiar and had taken on both bear and lion successfully. He had something even more important, though. He did not have to put on Saul's equipment because he had already taken up the most important armor available to him: his faith and conviction that God would carry him through.

Even today, although we may never face a bear or lion in up-close and personal combat, we still have an Enemy capable of killing our hope and stealing those precious possessions we try to guard. God loves each of us enough to equip us with our own specialized armor because He is truly in the outfitting business. In fact, you might say He is the ultimate outfitter because He deals in only the very best equipment and it is guaranteed for life—and beyond.

You see, when Scripture says put on the full armor of God, it is not a call to occasional accoutrement, like a costume to be taken out and worn when the occasion is right. We are not asked to take it off—only to take it up. To "put on the full armor of God" is a statement presented in such a way that David would have fully understood its intent. While wearing this armor we will surely be tested, and thus we need to get used to its fit while having faith in its testing. David understood it and staked not only his life but in effect the lives of all Israel that day on the outcome. God provides us with armor that is battle tested, so who would want to put on anything else? Go with the outfitter whose record is, well, impossible to beat.

9

Boundary Stones

Do not move the ancient boundary which your fathers have set. (Proverbs 22:28)

I love hunting old homestead farms. You never know what will pop up while exploring the thickets and fields. One outstanding hunting property, whose owner is more than happy to let me take kids out so they can enjoy the outdoors, is heavily overgrown and just about impossible to hunt in some places because it is so overgrown. Deer and turkey have abundant sanctuary there, which is why this place is so good.

It was a gorgeous spring morning, and three of us, youth hunter included, were chasing a gobbling bird who answered calls heartily but did not seem interested enough to turn around and come back. We moved after him slowly and steadily through cedar thickets and heavy brome. At the top of the rise, we knew the thick stuff would open up into what ten years before was a plowed field. Now it held nothing but emerging plum thickets and deer trails. Between us and the field lay a surprise I had not encountered before, having never ventured onto this part of the farm. A long, low stone wall stretched through the shadows. It would have been invisible even in overhead Google shots, but on the ground one of the homestead's old secrets was revealed.

This was clearly a boundary, and likely the stones dredged up from plowing the field above found a useful role to play in its construction. It was a wall of uniform substance along its length, perhaps two feet wide and three feet tall, and clearly not built without a great deal of effort. It had endured for many decades, serving a purpose that was perhaps no longer evident, but all the same, its character remained unchanged.

I liked it. I wanted to stop right there, take a seat on it, and just contemplate its existence, wonder about the hands that built it, and see if in the silence the wall would tell me any stories. However, any reflection would have to wait for another time. Fading gobbles and an expectant thirteen-year-old hunter demanded we press on.

The wall stayed in my thoughts long after the hunt concluded that day, and it has come to symbolize more than just some forgotten field boundary created from rocks that were an obstacle for the plow. It remains solid and unmoving and says very clearly, "Cross me, but only with effort." One could not accidentally breach it along its entirety even today, any such act having to be entirely willful. And therein lies the lesson.

These boundary stones are a metaphor for the old ways this country once represented—firm values, family traditions, and well-established boundaries that perhaps should not be changed. Yet today we discard long-honored social and moral limits as if they existed merely for such an eventuality, as if change for its own sake was actually a good thing, without a thought to why such boundaries might have endured not for decades but centuries. And we lose something valuable in the process. Perhaps it is a link to our forefathers or just devolution from when life was simpler and choices more clear. Whatever it may mean for those of us who value constancy over change, perhaps there are boundaries we should not challenge.

Perhaps, as the book of Proverbs notes, we should be careful when attempting to move those ancient boundary stones. Certainly we can, but will we ever be able to reform the boundary to what it once was, and at what cost?

10

Tracks in the Snow

"Come now, and let us reason together," says the
LORD, "Though your sins are as scarlet, they will be
as white as snow; Though they are red like crimson,
they will be like wool. (Isaiah 1:18)

The LORD's lovingkindnesses indeed never cease,
for His compassions never fail. *They* are new every
morning; great is Your faithfulness. (Lamentations
3:22–23)

I know a lady who lives by herself on a large tract of land.
We met via a mutual friend who knew the landowner needed
help with her coyote problem. I've been trying my best but
haven't made much of a dent in the population, which means
her chickens and ducks remain in peril. The last two times I've
been to her property, the field to the east of the house has been
blanketed in a fresh white sheet of snow.

The unspoiled snow enabled a very thorough yet quick scouting job, showing where the active routes across her property were and what sorts of animals were using them. A fresh snow will reveal secrets that would be virtually impossible to discern on hard, dry ground. Tracks in the snow provide evidence of activity; otherwise a searcher would only be met with a clean, trackless, and pure blanket of white.

If one searches the Scripture for references to snow, there are few, an understandable fact considering snow in that region of the world is a rarity. The advent of snow would be a singular and significant occasion, not an everyday event. Synonymous with snow is also the aspect of purity. It is white, clean, and unblemished and thus an image that resonates with believers, as only through Christ's blood are we washed white as snow, having the blemish of our sins removed.

It was this aspect that struck me the last time I went through her field. When I looked in front of me, I enjoyed the sight of a smooth, unmarked white blanket. Looking behind me, the view was no longer pristine, having been scarred by the tracks of our little hunting party on this day. At that moment I realized the snow was more than just a metaphor for purity. In God we are new every morning, and in the same way He wants our hearts to be as pure as a fresh blanket of snow. Every day we awake and make decisions on our own to plunge into the field of life that lies before us, yet we remain oblivious or perhaps unthinking about the tracks left behind. Those tracks represent our choices, actions that must be taken throughout the day but some not always with pure intentions or prayerful consideration.

I remain comforted by the fact that my God loves me so much that He will erase the tracks that lead in the wrong direction after a simple petition. He gives us the opportunity for fresh starts all the time, so perhaps every once in a while we should turn around, look back, and see if we like what we see. Or is it time to look ahead to that trackless blanket of pure white that God can offer us if only we ask?

11

Decisions on the Edge of Darkness

"They make night into day, *saying*, 'The light is near,' in the presence of darkness. If I look for Sheol as my home, I make my bed in the darkness; If I call to the pit, 'You are my father'; To the worm, 'my mother and my sister'; Where now is my hope? And who regards my hope?" (Job 17:12–15)

There are times when I wonder if we don't respect the darkness anymore. To the ancients the difference between light and dark marked a very clear divide. What was out there in the darkness made one respect the comforts of the campfire and the sanctity and protection of the walled shelter.

Today the divide no really longer exists, at least not the physical one. We can illuminate the darkness. We can subdue it and push it back with electricity and high-beam headlights. We seek to eliminate the darkness of misunderstanding with the tools of science. But neither science nor electricity can alter the nature of that darkness.

Darkness is more than just the inability to see; it marks the abode of evil. Only with light do clarity, comfort, and goodness come. In attempting to extend the boundaries of light and of knowing, it is still an inevitability that we encounter that band that is the twilight, something to which your eyes cannot adjust fully and that your mind cannot comprehend clearly. What happens? Those actions you choose to take on the edge of darkness can become questionable. If you are a hunter, these moments mark the difference between a clean shot and a bad one, an ethical versus unethical choice, and perhaps mark the difference between a quick kill and a long, arduous recovery.

How can a hunter take a shot if he cannot see? I have on many occasions passed up shots because my understanding of the situation would not allow it even though I was still on the legal side of shooting light. In the near dark, we can hear perhaps more clearly, our senses tuned to sound in the absence of unambiguous sight, but without sight we lack the understanding necessary to take the best shot. Only light can help us complete the picture.

We are challenged daily and put to the test of our actions in the home or workplace. The challenge then is to be clearly guided in our actions not only by the light of day but by the light of God's Word, thus allowing us take the best shot. In the same way electricity and science attempt to push back the darkness, society attempts to push back limits on what darkness is, recasting it as the current music fad or the latest hit movie or show, ultimately leading to a casual disrespect for the dark side of things. It has become all too easy to post things on the web that would not even be considered face-to-face. We can all too easily become what we are not in those twilight situations rather than who we are called to be.

So when you are facing that choice and feel compelled to pull the trigger on an action this week at work or home, if you are approaching the edge of twilight, make sure that not only is it legal light but that God's Word also informs your sight picture. Beware the dark.

12

Action Cam Pharisees

"When you pray, you are not to be like the hypocrites; for they love to stand and pray in the synagogues and on the street corners so that they may be seen by men. Truly I say to you, they have their reward in full." (Matthew 6:5)

I found myself—yet again—in the electronics section of the store lusting over those cool little action cameras that allow you to film your hunts in high definition. And for as many times as I have done that, that little guy on my shoulder who is my conscience ends up whispering, "Don't give in. You don't need it!"

Once again the little guy's prodding weighed supreme, and I left the store without making a purchase. Yet I remained bothered a bit that on my next exciting hunt, I would only be able to regale my friends with my version of how many points that buck had or how big the fish was. The sometimes-unbelievable stuff that goes on in the woods would be only between myself and the data stored in the gray matter of the hard drive that is my brain. What good is all that if all you have is a story and your friends can taunt you with video clips of their latest trip afield?

I have come to believe that some efforts to broadcast those adventures, while it may sound fun, can make you cross a fine line between self-enjoyment and self-promotion. The Pharisees fell into the same trap, and they might be the guys who just had to have one of those HD cameras. That would help them in their mission of proclaiming on the street corners that they were great men of God and had the footage to prove it.

I believe that no matter what we may put out there in the electronic realm, God sees it all differently, and in the end He's *the* guy who really matters. As long as we're having fun with what we do and don't hurt anybody, that HD stuff is just fine. When you cross a line of ethics in order to get that exceptional experience on camera by doing something you know you shouldn't, then welcome to the world of the Pharisees.

After all, those HD cameras don't make us better hunters. Only learning the lessons available in the woods can really do that. Neither can watching other Christians necessarily make us better unless we choose to act according to God's Word.

13

Unexpected Gifts

Do not boast about tomorrow, for you do not know what a day may bring forth. (Proverbs 27:1)

But God said to him, "You fool! This *very* night your soul is required of you; and *now* who will own what you have prepared?" (Luke 12:20)

The sightings were over thirty years apart. I was a neophyte waterfowl hunter in Oklahoma the first time I spied them while jump shooting ducks. They were just two large white birds in the shallows of a large lake, too far for anyone to tell accurately what they were, but my immediate hope was, "Snow geese!" They looked like snows, and since it was goose season, I connected the dots far too quickly and surmised that big white birds on a lake during goose season actually equated to snows. I crouched in the bushes and waited in the hopes that they would give me a shot if they ever took off.

After an interminable wait, they took flight and proceeded to come right over where I was hiding. Just as I prepared to bag my first goose, the recesses of my brain started to shout, "Whoa—take a closer look!" Even though I had imagined these birds to be snows, they were awfully darn large. In fact they were supersized, like feathered jumbo jets, and lacking the black wingtips of a typical snow goose. Upon recognition, I found myself marveling at my first-ever sighting of trumpeter swans. I had read about them and seen pictures and knew they were seriously endangered, but to see them in the wild was totally unexpected. Growing up in California meant never seeing things like this. I was certainly not prepared for the encounter.

They flew directly overhead not twenty yards above me. As they departed to the south, I realize my hunting for this day was done. They were an awesome note to end the morning on. At the time of my first sighting in 1980, there were not many breeding pairs of trumpeters in the United States, since the species was only beginning to recover from near extinction in the early '40s. I was left to ponder their departure in silent awe, knowing God had just sent me a singular gift for this season. I would not see any trumpeter swans again in the wild until thirty-four years later.

Fast forward to just after Christmas 2013, and my youngest son and I had driven to a nearby farm to try our hand at bow hunting for deer. We were parked at the top of a small rise surrounded by corn and soybean fields, busily stuffing ourselves into our cold-weather suits, when it happened.

December in Kansas can be awfully brutal, and this day marked no exception. Canada geese were flying all over, and I found myself looking skyward to watch the show while I struggled with my insulated coveralls. The birds were making an awful racket, but some of them sounded quite odd, hoarse almost. When I looked for the source of the noise, I found twelve trumpeter swans coming over not thirty yards distant, directly over Seth's shoulder.

I hollered at him, saying, "Take a look, buddy, as you don't see those every day."

He didn't seem nearly as excited as I was, but Seth is practiced in the art of cool. My infantry soldier son would only allow that they were pretty neat looking and very big. As I was still standing in the frigid air looking at the shrinking swans with my mouth agape like a fool, I can only hope that he realized he perhaps should have been more suitably impressed—with the birds, not me.

It turned out to be a season of trumpeter swans aplenty for us both, since we saw some just about every time we went to that farm over the next ten days. We weren't very far off the Missouri River, and it was sure neat to see these groups of birds trading about with the geese in the late afternoon.

For me these birds were an unexpected gift, and I reveled in each and every flight. I felt as if God had presented me with a great sight to feast my eyes upon, especially knowing how rare they had been not very long ago. I did not go afield expecting even remotely to see them, and yet there they were for the first time in decades. Magnificent and huge, a commanding presence not only with their size but also their attention-getting trumpeting, which reminded me of an old-style car horn in the distance. For me these were moments to treasure, not only because of the rarity and magnificence of the birds, but now they were also a sweet reminder of time afield with my son should I ever see trumpeters again.

God's gifts are like these moments. We cannot schedule the timing any more than we can the falling of rain or the arrival of the spring migration. These are God's to bestow, and I for one am thankful to be able experience such gifts, and even more so enjoy the extreme reverence when God hangs some of His most wonderful creations just a few yards up in the air for a sinner like me to enjoy. So the next time you find yourself gaping at something awesome God has chosen to bless you with, enjoy it. Revel in it. Acknowledge and appreciate it, because it might not happen for another thirty years. Tomorrow is not promised.

14

Two Stands

He who is faithful in a very little thing is faithful
also in much; and he who is unrighteous in a very
little thing is unrighteous also in much. (Luke 16:10)

There were two tree stands on private property that supposedly
only I had access to. I found them at season's end, nestled
into the trees on a part of the property I had not yet ventured.
It was evident the stands had been placed some time during
the months before I had started hunting there, as one was
new and neither showed signs of abandonment. Someone had
acted neither responsibly nor with respect. Having always
made it a habit to be respectful of the property of others,
finding these stands made me a bit angry. At a minimum
the presence of these two stands on private property was
unethical and at a maximum it was even a violation of law.

Either way, the new owner's nonresident situation had been taken advantage of.

The owner resided on another continent, in another country, many time zones away. I had encouraged him to let me frequent the place in order to show a little activity that might perhaps prevent the unauthorized use of the place, but this action was evidently too late. The property had been up for sale some time before the current owner had purchased it and was fenced but not gated. It was clear the circumstances invited issues, in this case perhaps someone knowingly taking advantage of the situation, thinking nothing would come of it. I surmised the stands belonged to the former property owner, who put them up knowing full well nobody would be along to check. While some may think this only a little indiscretion, to me it represented a resounding act of unfaithfulness.

When the situation involves matters of trust and law but no simple solution, what is one to do? Our lives can be like this. Unwarranted issues intrude, such as demands for our time or something we might be able to offer because of our position or authority. They steal into the property of our minds and souls unbidden, without permission. At times such an intrusion can even leave some feeling a bit violated, similar to my reaction upon finding those stands. They can influence us to perhaps make a bad choice or two, allowing our circumstances to invite issues that, absent an unwarranted intrusion, we might not have come up with on our own. Well-meaning friends may encourage you, "Go ahead, no one is watching," or "Who's counting? Not me."

The bottom line is we must be careful of what we allow in and know that there will always be those whose inability to be faithful in even the little things—like respecting the property of others—will inevitably lead them to fall short when counted on for something truly important. Never hang your stand where it isn't allowed or ask it of another. It may seem a small thing, but in matters of character, your own stand is the one that matters to God.

15

Poorly Aimed Shots

Death and life are in the power of the tongue, and those who love it will eat its fruit. (Proverbs 18:21)

He who restrains his words has knowledge, and he who has a cool spirit is a man of understanding. (Proverbs 17:27)

The brain is a marvelous computer. I knew milliseconds after the trigger broke to initiate the firing sequence to launch a high-powered bullet at a nice buck that I had missed the shot. I was still settling the crosshairs on the deer, and although he wasn't moving and presented a good broadside shot, I ended up whiffing on my only good opportunity of the rifle season.

It was, as countless mental replays would confirm even months later, all my fault. My aim was not off; I had just missed. The rifle was one I had owned for thirty years and have shot a fair number of animals with. Practice, however, had been minimal since going to a range to hone my skills involved a major investment of time and gas, and the longer distance of the shot was something I was not used to. The deer was almost three hundred yards away, and since I didn't shoot much even at one hundred yards, my mental preparation was every bit as deficient as my physical preparation. I could only blame myself. This round was spent in the stand of large trees that provided a backdrop for the shot.

Words, like bullets, have a target and an impact point as well. Whoever came up with that little saying, "Sticks and stones can break my bones, but words will never hurt me" has not spent much time on the Internet and likely had a pretty small circle of friends. Even though we get a lot more practice with our daily conversations and should probably be able to effectively hit what we aim our speech at, poorly considered words can be just like that bullet I launched. I couldn't call that 150-grain Nosler back, and neither can any of us call back words uttered in haste or anger. Bullets and words both can miss the mark. A missed whitetail will run off, but missing the mark on words can leave a lasting impact on someone you love.

Perhaps if we considered this parallel a little more often, we might be more deliberate in our choice of words—especially with those whose relationships we value. We live in an age of unparalleled communication capability, and there seems to be no shortage of opportunities to share an opinion on a blog site, fire off a hasty e-mail, or comment on someone's Facebook page, but we seem to have forgotten that not everything we say is really important. We want others to hear us lest our voices be unheard, and thus broadcast a lot, but it is often fire and forget.

Proverbs notes that the tongue has the power of life and death. A bullet has only one purpose; not so the tongue. Perhaps we should consider the outcome of firing verbal salvos and strive to send healing instead. Practice makes perfect.

16

More Thoughts on Habitat

> This command I entrust to you, Timothy, *my* son,
> in accordance with the prophecies previously made
> concerning you, that by them you fight the good
> fight, [19] keeping faith and a good conscience, which
> some have rejected and suffered shipwreck in regard
> to their faith. (1 Timothy 1:18–19)

If you are anything like me, you might be a bit of a dreamer. My dream is to someday purchase and manage my own little quarter section (160 acres) of hunting and fishing paradise. Thus I am forever on the lookout for that perfect parcel when I find myself driving around the local countryside. My eye is trained now to pick out "For Sale" signs and to identify those really likely parcels should they ever pop on the market.

Maybe you're just like me and have a finely honed ability to assess and mentally catalog every likely property you pass … when you should be paying attention to your driving. But probably you are not. It would be very difficult to match the years of practice I have at this endeavor. There is also that membership in a hunting club that affords me access to all sorts of different properties that I invariably evaluate as to suitability. I even have developed a score sheet to compare all the different properties surveyed. Sadly, all my looking and even the use of a highly developed score sheet has not helped. Years after starting my quest, I'm still looking for that perfect habitat. Some money to afford it all would be nice too, but when that PWPP (property with perfect potential) pops up, I'm prepared to sacrifice. In the meantime, the quest continues.

Big is not always better, and looks can be very deceiving. Drives through the countryside while wistfully looking at possibilities always seems to turn up one or two that just have "that look." There are other places that conversely appear quite unproductive but are actually loaded with wild game. Why is that? The usual good habitat suspects, such as food, water, shelter, and hunting pressure, come to mind, but these are difficult to measure from the road. Hmmm, that property three miles back looked like a sure winner though. Did it have *everything*? Hard to tell when you're flashing by at sixty-five miles per hour.

Looks can be deceiving, for I have discovered that if you actually spend time on some of these really superb-looking properties, they aren't all that productive. Sure, they hold game, but how come other folks in nearby locations always seem to do better? Maybe you haven't taken careful enough look at your habitat or spent enough time and effort to develop it properly. Usually good habitat results not from finding the perfect place but from acquiring land with potential and then working to develop it to the fullest. There is always effort involved.

We can ask the same question as to what is a suitable Christian habitat. Have you ever found yourself on a quest for the right Christian environment? What about the right Christian friends, or even the right church? If you have any experience with multiple assignment moves in the military, a constant challenge is finding a home and church family at a new post. This invariably means the family ends up driving around the countryside, looking for that other PWPP for your brood.

Not just any church will do, and neither will just any set of friends or neighbors, the latter invariably defined as kids next door who are the same ages as yours but perhaps may possess certain qualities you would rather your kids not be exposed to. So what do we need not just to survive but thrive in our environment, to develop our full Christian potential?

In real estate the mantra for sales is "location, location, location." For a Christian that location ultimately centers on the church. Most of the time, though, just being in a church is not all we may need, as it will only meet some of your family's requirements. In the same way, just being in the right neighborhood does not always guarantee you will have good neighbors with well-mannered kids yours could learn a thing or two from. What can we do about that? Regarding the subject of hunting property, there are always ways to improve the habitat and manage it for more higher-quality game. How can you do that in your neighborhood, town, or church?

Every Timothy needs a Paul, and every hunter or fishermen needs one as well. I was self-taught in woodsmanship since my dad thought hunting and fishing was just a big waste of time. The folks I hang out with today refer to an upbringing like this as form of child abuse. I still tend to do okay in the woods despite my lack of parental tutelage but only by having invested heavily in my formative years by reading every copy of *Field and Stream* and *Outdoor Life* I could lay my hands on. I learned by watching TV and by reading books as well, but there weren't very many people around to show me the way. I needed a Paul, but there were none.

Being a whitetail hunter adds a certain degree of difficulty, since hunting out of a tree stand is pretty much a singular endeavor. It doesn't have to be. You can teach what you know to someone else who might share your passion but not your knowledge. Take a stand and cultivate some heart habitat whenever and wherever you can. Gift others with your ability to tie a fly, make a roll cast, turn a turkey fan and beard into a wall mount, or find the best location to hang a stand. Encourage other outdoorsmen, and boys, and girls, and in turn you might find that your own Christian habitat suddenly looks a lot better, is more productive, and is the place others envision as their own ideal for that perfect "location, location, location."

17

Flailing with a Fly Rod

To the weak I became weak, that I might win the weak; I have become all things to all men, so that I may by all means save some. I do all things for the sake of the gospel, so that I may become a fellow partaker of it. Do you not know that those who run in a race all run, but *only* one receives the prize? Run in such a way that you may win. Everyone who competes in the games exercises self-control in all things. They then *do it* to receive a perishable wreath, but we an imperishable. Therefore I run in such a way, as not without aim; I box in such a way, as not beating the air; but I discipline my body and make it my slave, so that, after I have preached to others, I myself will not be disqualified. (1 Corinthians 9:22–27)

As a fly fisherman, I always found practice to be an endeavor of inestimable value. When I was a teenager, I would practice often in the backyard. The space was large enough to be able to cast as far as I wanted, as often as I wanted, without worrying about too many obstacles—except for the large oaks ringing the yard and fruit trees in Dad's little orchard. Okay, maybe I spent a lot of time unwrapping my line from the trees early on, but I learned along the way. It was here that I learned to load the rod and use its power for more distance, how to throw the line into the wind, how to keep the line flat when I needed to reach a target under an overhang, and how to accomplish a roll cast in order to avoid wrapping line in the trees lurking behind.

Of course, I had no hook on the leader when I practiced, and to the golfers who were passing by, I might have appeared to be just flailing at the air. But in fact I was honing my skills for those meaningful times when I would actually put them to use. So it was that I went from being an ineffective fly caster to someone who considered himself a virtuoso. I prided myself in never getting skunked and quite honestly cannot recall having an outing where I did not catch at least a dozen fish. I also enjoyed the attention that accompanied my evident proficiency. When you're a teenager and accomplish something that earns the respect of others, it has a profound impact. You become focused and earnestly seek the prize, whatever it may be, that comes with a strict training regimen required to get you to the top.

Those hours of practice paid off when I experienced hundred-fish days. It paid off when, as a seventeen-year-old kid, I went to a large public water and fished a heavily pressured stretch in plain sight of the local store on the main road. I was in the zone that day, that rare place where you achieve a form of Nirvana and everything around you goes blank except for the rhythm of the casting and the setting of the hook. I was oblivious to a small crowd that had formed behind me to watch. I also was oblivious to the anglers on my right and left. When

I finally noticed them, they evinced a mix of admiration and peevishness, experiencing their own apparently fishless efforts and wondering how a kid could have such success with such a silly-looking technique.

I would like to say I practice God's Word as much as the skills required of my hobbies—that I pursue the prize as eagerly as when I was a kid learning to fly fish. I would like to say that I can employ God's Word as easily as I can summon a roll cast in tight quarters on a mountain stream. I do not, like some of my Scripture-spouting friends, possess the ability to impress too many folks with my scripture memory skills. It seems I have a much greater ability to remember how to tie an improved clinch knot than come up with the right Scripture when it is time to share my faith or offer up the best conclusion to a Scripture lesson. In those moments I can end up really flailing. I wrap my scriptural line around the overhanging trees and snag hooks into everything except where I want to place it. I might as well be beating the air meaninglessly.

Mastering God's Word is not as easy as fly fishing, but the prize is so much greater. I know what it took to become halfway decent at fly fishing when I was still in high school, so I know today that when I purpose to achieve a goal, I can succeed. I need to learn to run the race for God's Word and its understanding with even greater dedication and focus than any of my worldly avocations. Flailing in these waters is not an option.

18

Christian Pursuits

"Listen to me, you who pursue righteousness, who seek the Lord: Look to the rock from which you were hewn and to the quarry from which you were dug. Look to Abraham your father and to Sarah who gave birth to you in pain; when *he was but* one I called him, then I blessed him and multiplied him." (Isaiah 51:1–2)

Hunting is all about pursuit. When I first took up the sport, I was fixated, as most neophytes are, on success in the field and bringing home a prize to be able to brag about. It was all about a photo to whip out of the wallet and something to hang on the wall. This, after all, was the point of the pursuit, was it not?

At some juncture, that all changed. Hunting became not about putting something in the truck bed but pursuing knowledge of the sport itself, to learn the woods and game and become woods wise. I took up archery not in the hopes of bagging more game but so the endeavor would make me better. The evolution of my ability was not measured in days or weeks but years. I find myself hunting harder each year, and while successes still come sparingly, I have learned so much that I've never regretted the decision. I also know I will never become a perfect hunter even with a rifle despite my progress with stick and string. That's okay by me because it's not always about success but what you learn along the way.

Sometimes, in talking with friends, we are led to discuss what is wrong with the church. There is so much in today's society that is not uplifting or appealing to Christians. If that's the case, there should be fewer excuses and more reasons to get involved with the church, where all the uplifting and appealing stuff should exist in multitudes! However, this is not what seems to happen. We do not find church to be an empowering event. Instead it is a series of little events, ministries, and classes that all aim to "fix" our failures as Christians. Having had more than a little experience in the army with both failure and success, especially in an environment that valued a zero-defects mentality, I'm of the belief today that God does not call us to lead faultless lives. I believe He calls us to lead effective lives. The question is, "How do we do that"? How can we overcome paralysis our efforts to live a faultless existence impose and instead embrace actions that involve risk and yet impact others?

David is a prime example. He made some awfully good decisions and conducted himself bravely on the battlefield. He also made some horrible decisions and conducted himself in a cowardly manner in his personal life. He fell down spiritually, morally, and as a leader. And yet he overcame these shortcomings and continued to serve God. His human nature challenged him, but his godly calling pulled him along. His example is an object lesson for all of us.

Just like my dogged pursuit of bow hunting to become a better hunter, I realize that it came down to a simple decision. I must pursue. As a Christian, I must pursue a relationship with my Creator and in that relationship find meaning. To establish a relationship with Christ merely to achieve eternal salvation is as hollow as it gets. You need to track Him down through the brambles, thickets, and deadfalls of your life. Along the way, expect to stumble and occasionally fall. If you do, get up and keep striving. In that you will find meaning. You will learn from that relationship, pursued over the course of a lifetime, not what it is to be faultless but to be effective.

19

Rhythm

There is an appointed time for everything. And
there is a time for every event under heaven.
(Ecclesiastes 3:1)

The rhythm of nature is easy to understand. It has a drumbeat
all its own that we can recognize if we pause long enough to
appreciate it. The hustle and bustle of our modern, instant
gratification society has caused us to lose touch with our
rhythm as a nation bit by bit. It happened slowly at first but with
increasing rapidity in the quickly changing information age
that has increased not only the speed of life but also the speed
of dissatisfaction—and the scope of its dissemination as well.

The educated opinions of trusted sages like Billy Graham,
Ronald Reagan, or Norman Vincent Peale do not resonate as
they once did. In their absence we have been released as a
people to explore the impact of our own ill-informed opinions,
and seem willing—in fact compelled—to comment on

anything and everything since we can so easily post on a blog or Facebook. Our opinion must be heard, no matter what its inconsequentiality. So, as we seek our own way, we lose touch with the rhythm of life. Misguided souls who feel only their opinion is worthy of a righteous crusade are out of touch and care not. Life's rhythm becomes not something to enjoy but to shape and create to your likeness. At times you can hear the trite saying to describe someone who "marches to the beat of his own drum." These days it seems everyone feels imminently qualified to do that.

Americans will say it's an expression of their freedom. It is their right, and it's guaranteed in the Constitution. That may be true but perhaps, the message has been skewed. How arrogant and how naïve that humankind seeks to establish its own rhythm. It is also curiously very natural. We are created in God's own image, and because of that we possess the same desire to create. After all, God creates, and so can we. So we seek to create our own rhythm, as if anything we come up with will be better than the original.

There can be only one Picasso, one Einstein, and one Mozart. Too much of anything means it is no longer special, unique, or out of the ordinary. Instead, a multitude of rhythms becomes just noise. It is a cacophony, an unwelcome assault on the senses. Read the headlines today and it is beyond that—it is vulgar, crass, and very this-worldly.

If you spend any time in nature, you'll find the problem with rhythm does not exist in the wild places. There may be a riot of noise, but it is somehow harmonious, pleasing, and soothing. Nature has rhythm. Nature knows when it is time.

There's a rhythm in the life of the animals, the rising in the setting of the sun and the changing of the seasons. It is a rhythm that has existed since the dawn of time. It is that sense of rhythm, the security and steadfastness of it that calls us to seek the wild places. Nature is God's retreat for us from the noise on the streets of Babel—where in our newly created town all do not speak the same language but each speaks only his own. Stay too long in its embrace and your soul will be affected. The siren song will draw you in, away from the sweetness of God's creation and into an alternate world of distaste that, if you allow it, will overcome your own senses and convince you all is good in the little world you created.

If that's where you find yourself, believing the reality you have created is the essence of life itself, it may be an Ecclesiastical time for you to ponder your circumstances, and seek a new rhythm.

20

Clothed in Majesty

The LORD reigns, he is robed in majesty; the LORD is robed in majesty and armed with strength; indeed, the world is established, firm and secure. Your throne was established long ago; you are from all eternity. (Psalm 93:1–2)

With appropriate credit to John Hart, creator of the comic strip BC, I still recall one exceptionally insightful cartoon from my childhood days. It dealt with the setting of the sun and offered a perfectly rational explanation as to why the orb got so big just before it went down. It was simple: "Look at all that daylight it has to suck up." For a twelve-year-old whose sense of humor and understanding of the universe was still developing, the image created in my mind was indelible. But sunsets are about more than just clever cartoons. They are the embodiment of majesty.

People of all backgrounds, nationalities, and ages can appreciate a beautiful sunset. Real estate deals are sealed because of the sunset views promised, millions of idyllic photographs are snapped annually, and the majesty of a day's end is a common subject of casual discussion in big cities and small towns the world over.

That is because something wonderful happens at sunset. The winds calm in anticipation, skies change dramatically, and the day shift of creation gives way to those who own the night. God bathes the land in a glow that is oh-so-special and in doing so reveals His majesty as He robes the earth.

Animals cannot appreciate the sanctity of the sunset. They were not created to do so. Only in mankind, the heart of God's creation, can daily worries be set aside in glorious anticipation of the loss of the day. So it is that only man can taste in his very soul the nocturnal approach and, concurrently anticipate the timeless resumption of the truth that is God—that God is the Creator.

Sunset paints the picture of a benevolent God kissing His creation good night. He repeats the bedtime story of His majesty in the perfection of sunset. He reaffirms that His throne is indeed established, as the Psalmist captured so eloquently in the verses that started this chapter. No matter what, the story goes, in the morning the sun will rise. A new day is promised. God has ordered the world, and to show His might and power, we enjoy the promise of the birth of a new day even as darkness beckons. God is mighty.

Likewise we anticipate the promise of a figurative renewal at sunrise. The anticipation is not hopeful but stridently faithful. We believe it will happen because God has established the world. Nothing humankind will do can change this truth inherent in the Psalm.

The next time you enjoy a glorious sunset in the solitude of the woods yet leave empty-handed, take care you do not leave empty. Rest in the knowledge that God demonstrated His love and His glory to you again, and you were a noble participant, a part of His creation clothed in majesty too. Take that home and be content. The Lord reigns.

21

Springs of the Great Deep

> In the six hundredth year of Noah's life, in the second month, on the seventeenth day of the month, on the same day all the fountains of the great deep burst open, and the floodgates of the sky were opened. The rain fell upon the earth for forty days and forty nights. (Genesis 7:11–12)

I learn more about this wonderful planet we inhabit all the time. Living in the Midwest, I always see farm ponds in my travels, and invariably those ponds were formed by building a dam across a creek drainage of some sort. Imprinted on my brain was thus the obvious fact that ponds are filled by runoff from rainwater.

I have a friend named Shawn with rural property that includes a modest pond his outdoorsy son can fish or swim in. Kansas suffered from drought conditions for the better part of two years and until recently, had been running behind on rainfall totals. A series of soft but steady drenching rains reversed that trend, and the water table has finally been replenished.

After the last of these rains, Shawn mentioned to me that he has to drive right by the pond to get to his home. He noted water had been flowing into it at a steady pace the evening before, yet the pond still was still not close to being filled. In the morning he encountered an entirely different scene, with the water level having risen close to four feet overnight and the pond at max capacity. Almost instantaneously the pond was full!

Now, considering his pond had never gone dry during our long drought, he deduced there was an underground water source feeding it—a spring. His son had confirmed it the day before our discussion while swimming, as he encountered a distinct thermocline in one area of the pond that was appreciably colder than the surrounding water.

Coincidentally, the very next day I was alerted to a scientific piece discussing the presence in the earth's core four hundred miles down that contain vast amounts of a material called ringwoodite, a water-bearing substance. The amount of water locked into this medium is potentially so vast that a scientist quoted in the article stated, "We should be grateful for this deep reservoir. If it wasn't there, it would be on the surface of the earth, and mountaintops would be the only land poking out."

Sound familiar? I think I read about this somewhere before, but usually scientific skeptics note that a flood just couldn't have happened, despite the presence of extremely similar "flood myths" that exist in numerous cultures! To tell the truth, I actually couldn't remember the part about the springs of the great deep in Genesis, so I went back to read it. Imagine that— there was confirmation of the two-pronged assault on dry land during Noah's time. Not just rain for forty days, which is the part that gets all the press, but the springs burst forth as well! The result was "only the mountaintops poking out."

The connection between a casual discussion and reading the results of a scientific report was almost mindboggling. In all my readings of Genesis, I had failed to appreciate the importance of God allowing the springs of the great deep to burst forth. Not just the deep, but the great deep. That a scientist would essentially confirm in 2014 what for many nonbelievers is a biblical myth—and with his comment verify with accuracy the precise wording found in Scripture—should be grounds for serious reflection. Rain alone was insufficient to cast Noah's ark afloat and raise it to the peak of Mount Ararat. Add the great springs bursting forth from four hundred miles below and the story is cast in a very different light.

My wife calls these little moments, when circumstance and information connect in order for me to gain a godly insight, "ooowie moments." I will never pass a farm pond again without considering that things are not always what they seem on the surface, that what my eye and brain "understand" may not represent the total picture, and that God always finds a way to surprise me. And this time He used a scientist. Will wonders never cease![1]

---

[1] http://www.newser.com/story/188387/400-miles-beneath-earths-surface-a-vast-ocean.html?utm_source=part&utm_medium=united&utm_campaign=rss_topnews; http://www.newscientist.com/article/dn25723-massive-ocean-discovered-towards-earths-core.html#.U53g4vldWOA

22

Navigational Errors

When the days were approaching for His ascension, He was determined to go to Jerusalem. (Luke 9:51)

What is your purpose for entering the woods? Perhaps it is to get away from troubles at the office or home and clear your head. Perhaps you've been waiting for months for an opening day that has finally arrived. It could be to honor a timeless family tradition or just the pursuit of a personal passion. But have you asked yourself about the purpose for which you really head to the wilderness, and once there, can you find your way through to achieve your ends?

It's rather easy to get lost once you lose sight of the road and your vehicle. If you spend any time at all in the woods, you have been turned around and found yourself questioning how to get back to where you started. Some folks seem to have no problems with this. They possess some innate capability to gauge direction, backtrack, and read the woods as easily as one might read a magazine. Today, of course, we don't even need that capability and can easily trade any semblance of woodsmanship for a global positioning system or GPS unit. But therein lies the purpose of the GPS—it shows us where we are.

Purpose, that intangible drive inside you, provides direction for your life. It can be likened to a directional needle, and in the conduct of our lives, this moral compass can keep us on clear track just as a GPS can lead us out of the woods, showing not only where we are but also in which direction to go. Seasoned woodsmen know to find a point on the horizon on which to orient. The same can be said for the moral compass inside us. In comparing the two, the inability to focus on what the needle is telling you can yield similar results—the user becomes lost. When navigating, those who don't keep track of targets on the distant horizon will instead focus on things closer in—and these are often the wrong things.

Allow just one undisciplined choice and you quickly move off track. Two wrong choices and you will be on the verge of being lost, in the woods as well as in life. For people, sometimes those bright, shiny objects get dangled in the way and take our own internal focus off the ultimate goal. Beware of the short-range waypoints that may look good but will get you lost in a big way in a short time. Take the long view. Fix your face on the target, and move with a purpose toward your eternal goal.

The man without a purpose is like a ship without a
rudder. A waif, a nothing, a no man. Have a purpose
in life, and, having it, throw such strength of mind
and muscle into your work as God has given you.

—Thomas Carlyle

23

Long-Lasting Impact

A gentle answer turns away wrath, but a harsh word
stirs up anger. (Proverbs 15:1)

If you have ever spent any time at all in a tree stand, you have
contemplated the distance from where you are way up a tree to
the ground below. It's interesting that an unexpected trip from
any such elevated position to the hospital, or worse, might be
only a matter of twelve feet.

A misstep resulting in a fall from a stand can, and will,
happen when least expected. Perhaps this is why there is
every bit as much emphasis on tree stand safety these days
as there used to be on gun safety when I was a kid. Each
stand sold comes with a safety harness, comprehensive use
instructions, and sometimes a wearer's use video. That's
because safety is a very big deal. If you fall, the results are

immediate. For that reason, I am extremely careful any time my feet leave the safety of terra firma as I climb up, stand on, or proceed down from a stand. I don't relish the idea of any injury that might result should I come face-to-face with the consequences of a mistake on the stand. If only there were something to absorb or deflect my fall, a soft pillow to fall into instead of perhaps blown-down trees, rocks, or just hard earth. It would be nicer than the alternatives. Perhaps that will be my get-rich-quick invention—a tree stand air bag that inflates upon impact! If it can be done for a Ford, why not a tree stand?

But that's just selfish thinking on my part, for what I want in the woods should I fall from a tree does not in any way reflect what others should be able to expect from me when they stumble around me, whether it is in any of my roles as a leader, father, or husband. I have never really been a soft place to land. When others have brought me a problem or failed to act as I feel they should, my responses have too often been too hard, too unreceptive, and all too ready to force my own judgment or response on others without my trying on God first. It is especially true in the workplace. We all know folks who appear to represent the epitome of that soft place on Sunday in public but become stone in the workplace or at home the rest of the week.

The world is full of folks like that, and every so often God puts that hard someone in my life when I'm hoping for exactly the opposite, when I think I need support and guidance, not fault-finding and prickliness. Deer season thus comes with many a subtle prompt about residual flaws in my own character. Like a string tied around my finger to remind me of something important, each trip up to the tree stand whispers to me that I should work harder on being a soft place to land. It doesn't mean I have to change my standards when others do wrong or have problems, only in how I receive the fallen.

24

Soft-Serve Ice Cream and Hope on the Arkansas

And not only this, but we also exult in our tribulations, knowing that tribulation brings about perseverance; and perseverance, proven character; and proven character, hope; and hope does not disappoint, because the love of God has been poured out within our hearts through the Holy Spirit who was given to us. (Romans 5:3–5)

We are an interesting lot, we men who fish—especially when we allow ourselves to dwell on expectations of what could be rather than drawing on experience. Hope seems to spring eternal in the breast of the ignorant, which explains why some of us are prone to launch forth on missions that the experienced would consider pure folly. It certainly explains why Adam, my sixteen-year-old, and I saddled up early one hot July morning to fish the headwaters of the Arkansas River in Colorado. We had not so much as driven by the area we were headed to fish, and I had never fished any sort of blue-ribbon water for trout. However, I assumed the fame of this particular stretch must mean that any fool could drive up there and catch trout until his or her arms got tired.

The morning sun found us waiting impatiently outside the local fly fishing shop on the banks of the Arkansas River in order to gear up and head north to the headwaters of this famed trout fishery. Yes, we were certainly hopeful, even more so because I had managed to break the tip on one of only two fly rods we had brought on the trip just the evening before. Hope—in the immediate—meant, "I hope they have a rod that doesn't cost an arm and a leg!"

I have fly fished since I was a teenager. In this regard my older brother was my idol as I got the inspiration and basic lessons from him. He still fishes avidly almost five decades later, taking at least one trip a year to fish famous waters that I've only managed to read about. I bore some small hope that at least when it comes to fly fishing, I could have a similar sort of effect on my oldest son and that he might take up my passion for the sport. It had certainly been a joy to introduce him to fly fishing during this family vacation. It would mark a return to normalcy for our entire family after living for five straight years abroad in countries like Egypt, where fly fishing was not even an option.

So on this particular day, hope won out over ignorance. We were fortunate enough that the outfitter opened early and even offered up a very good deal on a high-end five-weight rod with a matched reel, line, and all the backing. As I was excited to take my son on our daylong adventure for which we were now officially late, I was more than happy to pay the money (only an arm …) and hit the road for our two-hour trip north. We did not have the benefit of GPS or an iPad or manage to do any sort of Google search for some nice overheads of the stream before we went. Fortunately the road we were on paralleled the river, and we managed to find a very likely spot to pull over and park. We wasted no time grabbing our gear and getting down to the river. There were numerous trout rising, and it seemed that all we needed to do was start casting and we would be into fish in no time. We decided to split up to cover more of the stream and just enjoy the scenery and some solitude, and so we ventured forth with high hopes of plenty of fish and stories to tell back at the cabin once we returned.

The day remained hopeful but for all the promise the river tantalized us with, fishless. In that regard hope continued to win out handily over ignorance even as the hours stretched on and the sun got higher and hotter. Time passed without a fish being caught by me. I had cast, flailed, re-rigged with different nymphs and dry flies, hiked, slogged, and sweated my way down the river with nothing to show for my efforts except wet shoes—that and a nice, nearly new plastic water bottle someone had lost along the way. I decided to turn back and found my number-one son trekking along the river looking for me. He had thoroughly enjoyed the morning but had the same thing to show for his efforts—that was, a big fat zero in terms of fish action. Our hopes for fish were now outweighed by the promise of a nice soft-serve ice cream at the local soda shop on the way back into town. This seemed to be a pretty good compromise after five hours, as we were both very hot and tired. The sun can be extremely brutal when you are at eight thousand feet.

Hope, however, had not yet totally abandoned us. During the hike back to the car, Adam and I discussed our next moves as we went along and in doing so passed what seemed a very likely spot. The current was strong here and had undercut on the far side of the bank. The crystal-clear water rolled over large round stones and seemed to offer a very hopeful fishiness. It was exactly the type of place that the worthies wrote about in the high-end journals.

One could almost conjure up a vision of what it looked like below the current roiling the surface. Underneath there were some jumbled larger boulders and the occasional tree root or other obstacle behind which a large fish could lurk while waiting for a tasty morsel to drift by. Earlier I thought it held such promise that I passed it by in hopes that Adam might be able to take advantage of any unpressured fish holding in it. Adam explained that he had in fact fished here and thought he had a strike. Still being new to fly fishing, he couldn't be sure if it was that or just a snag, but he said his line had stopped briefly in the current. I took note of this, and it was at this moment that the student became a teacher. He said, "Dad, you should give it a try."

I took him up on the offer. Surely we could not have come all this way, to a real no-kidding blue-ribbon type of stream no less, and leave empty-handed. He coached me on my presentation and where to cast. His directions were very good for a novice, and I was proud I that he was such a quick study.

I thought to myself, *It would be so cool if I actually caught a fish with Adam's help.* My first cast set up a good drift but nothing happened. As I worked the line for the next cast, Adam said, "See if you can get it out closer to the deep cut."

I managed to do just that, and halfway through the drift, my line stopped. Although I was pretty much a novice myself at stream fishing, I'm not a big believer in coincidence. Adam's line had stopped too, right? Instinctively I raised the tip of my new untested rod and was instantly into the solid pressure of a good fish. Needless to say, excitement was high on the banks of the Arkansas River at that particular moment.

After an excellent fight from a fish that bulldogged the bottom as much as he could, I pulled into the slack shallow water a gorgeous brown trout. It was all of sixteen inches and perhaps even more. It was thick of body and its colors shone vividly in the bright Colorado sunlight. Had it been only six inches it still would've been a trophy of a lifetime for me. It remains a very precious memory—the result of a team effort that I hold to just as dearly years later. Perhaps I might be able to match this moment at some point in the future, although I doubt I can surpass it. We celebrated on the way back to the cabin with ice cream.

I guess that's the beautiful thing about hope. After all your efforts and with time running short, maybe the best you can hope for really is just a nice soft serve ice cream instead of fish. But maybe, just maybe, God will bless you with something precious, unexpected, and of everlasting value to your soul. Expectations were met—and exceeded—despite the lack of experience. Hope had indeed won out. This means that at some point in the future, when visions of some other adventure are placed into my head, I'll saddle up and find some unwitting person to go along, all the while hoping that whatever blue-ribbon road we are on will yield the hoped-for result. I'll just make sure to scout out the nearest ice cream parlor.

25

Kairos and Kronos

He said to them, "It is not for you to know times
or epochs which the Father has fixed by His own
authority." (Acts 1:7)

I am not a big believer in using trail cameras to assist my deer
hunting. It may be a foolish personal prohibition, but I do
not own a trail camera and have never had much of a desire
to use one. My time in the woods is about improving my
poor woodsmanship and connecting with God, not fretting
about technology and connecting with some remote spying
program. If I can't bag deer using my own skills, perhaps
I have no business blundering about the woods in the first
place. Technology is synonymous with kronos, known to the
ancients as one of the mythological Titans but more recently
recognizable as Father Time. It also represents the root of
the word *chronograph*, which my father would understand to

be his watch, that piece of technology that helps us to keep chronological tabs on our day.

Kairos is something entirely different. It represents God's timing and is not remotely synonymous with any sort of sequential or predictable time. I am always interested in discussions about deer and deer hunting, but somehow it seems a little too precise to pattern deer by using remote technology. If I wanted to, I could head out to my favorite sporting goods store and purchase a camera that would tell me what is going on in the woods while I am anywhere but there. I could be at the ball game and receive a text with a picture of an animal next to my camera. I could be getting ready for bed and have another alert. I could be in the midst of a business meeting and be informed remotely of activity in the woods. I would be able to gather an actual record of not only when animals are moving but also which specific animals are moving. Conversely, a lack of activity will tell me I have chosen poorly about where to place the camera.

Certainly much can be learned from all of this, but it's not exactly like real scouting. Glean enough information from your trail cameras and all you have to do is get a sense of correlation between activity and kronos and you can fairly easily put yourself in a position to harvest a respected big-game animal within a very precise window. Something about predictability and hunting makes for strange bedfellows in my mind.

Perhaps this is why I prefer the kairos way. It represents the provision of God's blessings and grace so much better because kairos is not about chronology at all. It is very simply an expression of God's timing in our lives. Thus to experience a moment of kairos in the woods is to synchronize with God's plan. I'm not in control of circumstances out there, and I don't set the agenda for the meeting. These are God's woods, and I prefer it God's way.

Conclusion

Counting Coup … and What Really Counts

After I completed the work on the short stories in this collection, I realized it lacked a final piece to pull it all together, a coup de grace, so to speak. This presented a small challenge since many of the stories are so different from the others. It was thus fitting that inspiration for the conclusion would occur on the margins of a church activity.

Following a recent sermon, we were all enjoying fellowship in the chapel greeting hall, and a close friend asked about my progress on the book. As usually happens with us, talk quickly turned to discussion of the ongoing deer season, one he was living out vicariously through me since his wife had recently given birth to triplets and any prospects of him going hunting were subsumed by Dad duties. I suspected these duties would keep him out of the woods for perhaps the next decade or so, and thus it was my solemn duty to at least give him a taste of what he was missing. I had a cool new piece of technology with me and was able show him a short video on my iPhone that he might appreciate. In it a small buck wandered within shooting range of my deer stand and stopped, offering a broadside archery shot, which I elected to pass on. I joked that this was the second time this little guy had given me a perfect shot and was able to walk away.

My friend, who has Native American Indian heritage, was taken back to his childhood by this and shared about his time as a young boy learning the practice of counting coup. For him it was a rite of passage to learn to get close enough to an animal to harvest it and yet allow it to live. He had chosen a deer as the animal on which he would perfect this art, which spoke a bit to me of his character since there were certainly easier marks he could have tried. In the old days, learning to count coup served a greater purpose of training up a young warrior. It seemed we had found something in common, and I was able to reflect back on the times I had also counted coup on animals I was supposed to be hunting.

I had taken up archery hunting long ago in the hopes of making myself a better hunter. In the process, I somehow became a better Christian. I learned to value God's lessons provided in forests and fields and walked away time and again richer for the experience. In talking with my friend, I realized I had counted coup on many an animal simply because in my evolution as an outdoorsman, the harvest did not represent my sole purpose for hunting. It was something else—something much deeper.

What really counted were the lessons harvested and many a fine adventure I was able to share with family and friends. These lessons provided me with the basis for the stories in *Wilderness Reflections*, which in their generation have profoundly deepened my own understanding of why I hunt and fish. In addition, the next animal I pass on I will make it an overt act of counting coup, thus honoring my friend, who will hopefully be afield somewhere with his triplets perhaps doing the very same thing. And ultimately I will honor God through it all, as it is He who provides me with the opportunity to practice stewardship. Will I make the right choices, and will my time in wilderness solitude count? Those are the tags I really want to fill, as they nourish my soul and strengthen the fiber of my being. That is something Jesus, from His sojourn in the wilderness, would understand.